# Who Is Elon Musk?

## What Do They Different to Succeed

The Story of a Boy Who Got Bullied In School and Then Went On to Become the Most Interesting and Famous Man in Tech

**By Phil Cooper**

*"The path to the CEO's office should not be through the CFO's office, and it should not be through the marketing department. It needs to be through engineering and design."*

**— Elon Musk**

**Who Is Elon Musk?**

This isn't some rags to riches story that will make you wonder how this guy made it happen. One thing that can be taken away from Elon Musk's successful history is that you should dream big and never let anyone crush or question your vision. Life has its ups and downs, and when the odds are stacked against you, no one will help you but yourself.

Elon Musk was just another kid in a classroom who was always thinking about making something unique. With his mind full of inventions he wanted to create, Elon became so lost in his daydreams that even his parents were worried he wasn't in the right frame of mind. However, Elon knew that one day his dreams would come true, and today, he's the 3rd richest man in the world after Bernard Arnault & Family and Jeff Bezos (The founder of Amazon). The places keep changing as the billionaires make more wealth and battle to rise to the top.

This eBook will take you through the life journey of Elon Musk and how he founded PayPal and became the CEO of Tesla and SpaceX. Along the way, you will learn his secrets to success, as well as get to know the advice he has for budding entrepreneurs who are trying to create a name for themselves.

# Table of Contents

# Introduction

If you want to truly know who Elon Must is, a visit to his SpaceX headquarters in Hawthorne, California, will reveal much about him. Visitors who enter that sanctuary see two giant posters displaying Mars in all its glory. They mark the pathway to Musk's cubicle.

So, why are these posters so important?

The poster on the left shows Mars as a barren land that is nothing but a red orb, and the poster on the right shows a green landmass surrounded by oceans. Mars has heat, and it's been transformed so that humans can live on this planet. That's the vision Musk has, and he fully intends to make it happen.

He believes that if we can develop a solution for sustainable energy, we would become a multi-planetary species that can survive on another planet and cope with worst-case scenarios that might threaten the human race's existence.

On June 28, Elon Musk hit another milestone — he turned 50. In the past five decades, Musk has accomplished the impossible. He became the CEO of SpaceX and Tesla, co-founded Neuralink and OpenAI, founded The Boring Company, and focused on his long-standing goal: leaving Earth and living on Mars.

If you think about it, the solar batteries, electric cars, space rockets, and the billions in wealth make Musk a real-life Tony Stark. If you didn't know, the inspiration behind the 2008 Marvel film "Iron Man" is Elon Musk.

Unlike other billionaires who flaunt their wealth, Musk is more focused on coming up with innovative solutions to make the world a better place. In January 2021, Tesla Owners of Silicon Valley tweeted, "@elonmusk is now the richest person in the world at $190 billion."

The CEO of Tesla responded to this with the following tweet:

"How strange" and "Well, back to work…"

This tweet provides great insight into what Musk thinks about his wealth. People call the SpaceX headquarters "Muskland," and it leaves visitors stunned with their mouths hanging open when they enter the building. The front is decorated with a 550,000-square-foot rectangle that says, "Unity of Body, Soul, and Mind" in white.

Though the building might be in a rundown neighborhood, the grandeur hits you in all its glory when the doors to the SpaceX building open. SpaceX has plenty of other buildings where multiple rockets are made at a time. Those who own Teslas can make their way to the parking lot outside the studio, where cars can be topped with electricity for free.

Despite all this, the *Muskian* nature of Elon is a bit hard to digest because he likes to control things around him. In 2015, an American business columnist Ashlee Vance wanted to write about the untold story of Elon Musk. After informing Musk about his intentions, he was told sternly that the billionaire wouldn't cooperate with him. After interviewing many of Musk's friends and current and former employees, Vance still hadn't learned anything new that couldn't be found on the internet. After 18 months of negotiations, Musk finally agreed to meet with Vance. He would cooperate with Vance as long as Musk got to read the book before it got published. Vance understood this request but, for various reasons, didn't comply.

He believed that Musk's truth would be a version of his perspective rather than that of all, which would not do justice to the story. However, he did agree to listen to Musk and take his side of the story under consideration.

And that's how the book *"Elon Musk – Tesla, SpaceX, and the Quest for a Fantastic Future"* was written.

# The Story of Elon Musk



Life is fickle. How many times have you heard this?

Things happen for a reason, but you can mold your story whichever way you like when you become the reason. All that's required is determination and hard work. Failure was, is, and always will be an option, so don't be afraid of it. When you fail, you learn because they say, "Try and try until you don't succeed."

That's how Elon Musk became the entrepreneur of the century and slowly made his way to the top!

Musk was born in 1971, on June 28, in Pretoria, South Africa. Like any other kid, Musk had big dreams that revolved around discovering something new. His habit of daydreaming got his parents worried, which prompted the doctors to order a hearing test.

Now we know that Musk's only disability was that he was allergic to taking advice that didn't encourage him.

When Musk was 10, he developed a deep love for computer science and technology. This change in him was due to his parents getting divorced. It was in 1984 when the public was first introduced to Elon Musk. He was 12 at the time. *PC and Office Technology*, a South African trade publication, got wind of the video game's source code Musk had designed. The science-fiction space game called "Blastar" required around 167 lines of commands to run; this was the time when a command needed to be typed for the computer to do a task. While his game did not shine as much as he had hoped, it sure beat the creations 12-year-olds were coming up with. When the game and Musk was covered by a Magazine, his worth netted $500. The game's spread, which was printed on page 69, showed a young man named E. R. Musk and his visions of conquests.

The game's description was, "You have to destroy an alien space freighter, which is carrying deadly Hydrogen Bombs and Status Beam Machines." Even at this young age, Musk was a remarkable and bright student. His ability to blend reality and fantasy helped him come up with the innovative ideas that bring in billions of dollars today.

Even though he became an inventor at the age of 12 and was featured in multiple publications, the world wasn't ready to accept him. With his first software out there in the world, he still had a long way to go. He knew the importance of education and dedicated most of his time to studying. As a bookish person and an introvert, Musk was bullied in grade school.

At age 14, Musk went through an existential crisis. As an adolescent but a gifted one, he tackled the situation like all other adolescents do — by turning to philosophical and religious texts. He sampled a few ideologies but ended up where he started and embraced sci-fi lessons. During this time, he learned that the only way a human being could think outside the box or step outside their comfort zone was by striving for greater enlightenment.

When he turned 15, he went through a growth spurt that allowed him to defend himself. While Musk was not the kind of person who liked confrontations or fights, he still learned how to wrestle and karate.

At the age of 17, Musk moved to Canada. In 1989, he attended Queen's University and avoided the South African military service that was mandatory after a certain age. During this year, Musk was able to secure his Canadian citizenship. He felt that with one citizenship in hand, he would easily obtain another one in the US.

In 1992, Musk went to the US to study physics and business at the University of Pennsylvania. After getting his undergraduate degree that was in economics, he stayed for another in physics. He still carried a hunger for education, so he enrolled in California's Stanford University for a Ph.D. in energy physics. It was in this year that Musk's luck shot up. The internet boom hit, and Musk dropped out of Stanford to launch his first company.

As a result, Zip2 Corporation was born in 1995.

**The Story of Zip2** began in 1994 when Musk was doing his internships. While working in the office, he had a chat with the Yellow Page's salesperson. Musk tried to pitch his idea of having an online listing along with the one on paper. The salesperson did not have much knowledge about the internet and how one used it to find business, and thus, he struggled to grasp the concept.

Although Musk's pitch was flimsy, he believed in it and decided to tell it to his brother Kimbal. Since Kimbal himself was into this line of work, he saw the potential in the idea, and both brothers decided to do something about it. That's when both brothers formed Global Link Information Network, which was later named Zip2.

Many businesses still had no idea how the internet could benefit a company, which is why they had no interest in getting a website created that would let them do *marketing online*, a concept that hadn't been born yet.

So, Musk and Kimbal hoped that establishments like clothing shops, hairdressers, and restaurants would see the benefit in it.

The concept of Zip2 was that it would create a business directory that was tied to the maps and would help people search different businesses and the directions to it. You might scoff at the idea now because we have Google Maps and Yelp, but no one could come up with this kind of service back then.

Zip2 was brought to life by the Musk brothers in Palo Alto at 430 Sherman Avenue. Since the brothers were still short on money at the time, they rented an apartment for the office, which was 20ft x 30ft, and got some basic furniture. The 3-story building where their business was housed had no elevators, and every now and then, the toilets would back up. According to Musk, it was a "shitty place" to start a business, but that's all they could afford at the time.

One thing that was necessary for their startup was a fast internet connection. So, Musk asked entrepreneur Ray Girouard, who also happened to be an internet service provider, and had the office on the downstairs floor to provide him with one.

Zip2's coding was handled by Musk, whereas Kimbal took control of the door-to-door sales. When everything was ready, Musk contacted Navteq, a company that created digital maps, and struck a bargain with them. Zip2 and Navteq merged their databases and created a rudimentary system. The company was started with $28,000, and by the time the maps were ready, both Musk and Kimbal were broke so they lived at the office.

They showered at the YMCA and ate 4 meals a day from Jack in the Box.

As time went on, Musk made more improvements in the code, and finally, they started hiring. They were still short on capital when an opportunity came knocking on his door. The CEO of a venture capital firm called Mohr Davidow Ventures caught wind of how two South African boys were making Yellow Pages for the internet. So, he asked them to come in with a presentation prepared. The CEO was so impressed with the idea they pitched that he invested $3 million into the company.

Zip2 then moved to a larger office and created a package targeting newspapers. The print media was slow to understand how the internet would help them, but they eventually saw its benefits and hopped on the Zip2 train.

This investment pushed Musk into the role of Chief Technology Officer, and Rich Sorkin was hired as the CEO of the company. Up to this day, Musk curses the moment he decided to give up his hold on Zip2 and made Sorkin the CEO. After a while, he felt that he had made a deal with the devil.

Problems started when the new hires started making changes in the code. Since Musk was a self-taught coder, his skills were no match with what the other engineers had. He bristled at the coding changes, but they were necessary as Musk's work was too complicated, and because of it, the software was liable to crashes.

As the company continued to climb successful heights, Musk felt that Zip2 was going in a completely different direction. The company had become all about catering to businesses rather than consumers. So, Musk decided to pitch the idea to buy a new domain name and market their services to consumers. However, Sorkin loved the fame and money they were getting from media companies. So, he decided to merge with CitySearch.com that offered somewhat the same services as Zip2. The merger was announced in the newspaper, and soon, the companies were faced with the difficult decision of which employees to keep and which to fire. Since CitySearch.com had a more talented team of engineers, Zip2 employees knew they would be sacked first. Musk, who was first in favor of the merger, turned against it.

What started in 1995 ended in 1998 when the merger was canceled. Musk called a board meeting and wanted the members to oust Sorkin and reinstate him as the SEO. However, the board refused, and Musk was demoted from his Chairman title. Later on, Sorkin was replaced by Derek Proudian.

Musk asked Proudian if he would back up his consumer-driven service idea, but the venture capitalist disagreed and said, "This is your first company, and now it's time for you to get an acquirer and start on your second, third, and fourth company."

Microsoft had already stepped foot in the market and was going in the same route. Proudian believed that investing any more money into the company would end in loss. In 1999, Compaq Computer offered to buy Zip2 for $307 million. Everyone agreed that this was the best way to recover from any loss they had faced so far.

Musk and Kimbal received $22 million and $15 million for their shares in the company, and they never looked back. With Zip2 sold, Musk moved on to his next project, and from there onwards, he decided to never relinquish the rights of being the CEO for any of his companies in the future.

The most important lesson that Musk took away from his first venture is that he could have handled things a little differently. Since he had never worked with a team before, he had no idea how to share or explain his vision to his colleagues. Employees would go home at night, and Musk would stay back, trying to improve the code. They would come in the morning and see all their work changed. Moreover, Musk was never good with an apology, and his confrontational style of speaking never sat well with any of the employees.

**The Story of PayPal** began in 1999. Musk was full of confidence after the sale of Zip2. He had learned a lot behind the lines and accomplished his dream of becoming a dot-com millionaire. Now, he was on the search for an industry that was falling behind and had inefficiencies but tons of money. He wanted to explore the world of the internet further, and after much thinking, he found the perfect target — banks.

As an intern, he had worked at the Bank of Nova Scotia. During his time there, he had learned that though bankers were rich, they were also dumb, and that presented a massive opportunity worth exploring. Back then, he was the Head of Strategy and asked to look at the third-world debt portfolio of the company. The money under this portfolio was labeled "less-developed country debt." Countries in South America and other continents had defaulted many times, which had forced the bank to not down the climbing debt. Musk was told to dig into the bank holdings and find out how much debt they were in.

This is where Musk stumbled upon the business opportunity and decided to do something about the debts that the US had. To lessen the debt burden, the US had introduced Brady Bonds that backstopped the debts of countries, such as Argentina and Brazil.

The arbitrage play didn't go unnoticed by Musk. The backstop value was at 50 cents, whereas the actual debt was being traded in at 25 cents.

Musk was all but jumping with joy to grab this opportunity with his hands, feet, and mind. He casually inquired about the Brazilian debt from a trader in the market. When asked about how much he wanted at 25 cents, he threw out the first number that came to his mind — $10 billion.

The trader said it would be doable, and Musk ended the call. He was aghast at what the trader had said because the money was backed by Uncle Sam. One summer, he had earned $14/hour and had gotten yelled at for using the coffee machine, which was reserved for the executives. With the talk he just had, the golden opportunity to shine was right in front of him. So, he ran up to his boss and said, "You can get your debt settled for free."

His boss told him to make a report, which was then passed to the CEO who promptly rejected it saying they had been burned too many times by Argentina and Brazil, and they didn't want to take any more chances.

Musk explained to them how they were backed by Uncle Sam, but the CEO still wouldn't listen to him. After the rejection, Musk considered opening his own internet bank and discussed it with his colleagues at Pinnacle Research. When he tried to convince the scientists of his ideas, no one was invested in it like he was, because they all believed it would take ages for internet security to be of top-notch quality for customers to trust it.

The plan that Musk had concocted was beyond anyone's imagination. People felt uncomfortable about buying books online, and here, Musk was planning to tell them that by entering their account numbers, they would get the advantage of online banking.

His plan was to build a financial institution that would have checking and saving accounts, and insurance and brokerage services. At that time, building this kind of technology was not impossible. However, rules and regulations of creating an online book, that too from scratch, were unheard of. But Musk, ever the optimist, knew he could do it. This was not a venture like Zip2, where all Musk had to do was provide directions. He was asking people to entrust him with their finances, and if anything were to happen to the services delivered, the repercussions could be devastating. Despite all the cons of his idea, Musk jumped into action.

Even before the sale of Zip2 had been finalized, Musk had started working on his new plan. He talked with the best engineers who had worked at Zip2 and even contacted his former colleagues from some of the banks in Canada.

It was in March 1999, Musk incorporated X.com. Being a finance start-up, the name sounded a bit pornographic but Musk was not worried about that. By now, he had earned a billionaire reputation and he reveled in the lavish lifestyle he had. He called CNN at 7 A.M. to witness the delivery of his McLaren, of which only 62 models existed in the world.

With his $22 million, he had become cocksure, and his flashy lines in front of the cameraman even made the crew cringe. He talked about his Zip2 deal and then led the audience watching from their houses to the X.com office.

Despite his antics, such as blowing up his McLaren, talking too much about money, and flashing his wealth around, Musk still didn't have a playboy persona. The majority of his millions, more than half of it, went into building X.com. In the end, he was left with $4 million for his personal use.

Musk invested about $12 million into X.com, leaving him, after taxes, with $4 million or so for personal use. "That's part of what separates Elon from mere mortals," said Ed Ho, the former Zip2 executive, who went on to cofound X.com. "He's willing to take an insane amount of personal risk. When you do a deal like that, it either pays off or you end up in a bus shelter somewhere."

One would say that Musk's decision to go almost all in was a huge mistake that could have resulted in him living in his car. However, he liked to take risks, more so than his investors. Zip2 had been a neat and clean idea but X.com had the potential to revolutionize the world.

One of the things that people came to know about Musk, which became his trademark, was that he always entered an ultra-complex business with plenty of planning but little knowledge about the industry's nuances. The fact that Musk embraced this showed that he didn't care the slightest.

Musk believed that bankers didn't know the intricacies of finance and that he had the power to run it better than them. His confidence and ego were so high that some people were inspired by it, and others thought of him as unscrupulous and pompous.

However, all that was about to be shut down because the creation of X.com would reveal Musk's foibles as a trailblazer, relentless drive, and creativity. We all know that with a great vision comes struggles and disappointments that leave a leader feeling unfulfilled. Musk had no idea, but once again, he world face the bitter reality of being pushed aside and others taking charge of his company.

Musk started assembling his team, which included qualified people from Zip2 and two finance expert Canadians. Their group of 4 was the cofounders of X.com, with Musk being the largest shareholder because of his huge upfront investment. All cofounders were on board from the start, agreeing with Musk's observation that banks had fallen behind in giving customers what they needed. Among them, only Musk knew the ins and outs of banking. The more the cofounders learned about how banks worked, the more they worried about the regulatory issues that would block their creation.

There were also many personality clashes. Fricker, one of the co-founders, wanted to make his mark on the world as a banking wizard. The visionary statements that Musk made didn't sit well with Fricker. He thought of them as silly because the company was still struggling to do anything. Soon, Musk and Fricker entered into an argument, which turned into a huge fight. Fricker had had enough of Musk's flighty thoughts and controlling behavior so he decided to start a coup.

He told Musk that he either let him take over as CEO or he will not take the employees with him and start a company of his own. Musk had never done well with blackmail so he tried to convince the employees to stay with him. His words went unheard, and some of the key engineers sided with Fricker. In the end, Musk was left with a handful of dedicated employees and a company that was nothing but a shell of its former self.

This didn't lower Musk's spirits. He simply decided to hire more employees. He approached a few more investors, one of which was Musk's friend. This friend decided to back him up even when the company was clearly falling apart. Musk had a different plan now. He hit the streets now with his speech on internet banking to attract as many engineers as he could. The plan worked and dozens of engineers joined the company to turn Musk's vision into reality. After a while, the company could secure a mutual fund license and banking license and strike a partnership with Barclays. At the end of 1998, the company had successfully created the first online bank that had FDIC insurance, which backed the bank accounts and multiple mutual funds people could choose from.

For the testing phase, Musk gave his employees $100,000, and on Thanksgiving, X.com finally went live. The company went into a battle with another company called Confinity that was offering the same services. When Confinity ran out of their cash reserve, Musk decided to form a merger, which made him the largest shareholder.

As X.com's customer base exploded, it became difficult for the website to keep up with the increasing demands. Every once in a while, the website would crash, and the ongoing competition from numerous startups caused Musk a lot of stress.

What Musk didn't know was that once again, people from his company were planning a coup! A few of his employees gathered one night to discuss how they could push Musk out of the company. These employees presented their idea to the board and propose that Thiel replace Musk. During this time, Musk had married and decided to go on a honeymoon trip with his wife. As he boarded the plane, letters were sent out about the board meeting, and people who were loyal to Musk could not believe that this was happening. One of his friends tried to call him, but Musk could not be reached. As Musk's plane landed back into the country, he got to know that he had been replaced from the position of CEO.

As the CEO, Thiel changed the company's name from X.com to PayPal in 2001, and Musk worked as an advisor, investing his money to take the company to the top. Most people thought that Musk would be bitter because of this change but he was quite supportive. As PayPal started getting huge, many giants approached with offers for a buyout. At the time, PayPal was making $240 million per year; so, Musk convinced the board to hold out for a bigger offer. Finally, in 2002, eBay offered $1.5 billion for PayPal, and the board accepted the offer.

It was Musk's guidance that allowed PayPal to survive for so many years even after the dot-com bubble burst. The company became a blockbuster IPO after the attacks of 9/11. Later, being sold to eBay for such an astronomical price, PayPal left a mark that no one can scratch even today.

**The Story of SpaceX** began in 2002. Musk had had enough of PayPal. After being removed as the CEO, he felt that there was nothing left in Silicon Valley for him. So, he decided to move somewhere more glitzy and glamorous. It was in Los Angeles that he found his calling for space. He felt that he was done with internet services. With his childhood fantasies of rocket ships revisiting him again, he changed courses again.

One night, when Musk and his employees were celebrating the sale of PayPal in Las Vegas, they noticed something different in him. Musk was openly talking about space travel and how it would change the world. The reason why Musk picked LA was that it had consistent, mild weather, which made it a favorite city of the aeronautics industry. Musk didn't have a plan in mind, but he knew that, in LA, he would be surrounded by top aeronautics thinkers, and that would give him the inspiration he needed.

Musk first interacted with aeronauts when he met a group of people, who were space enthusiasts and members of the Mars Society, which was a non-profit group. This society was dedicated to exploring the Red Planet and held a fundraiser for it in 2001. The event's invite was $500/plate and was sent out to the usual people in the community.

What no one expected, including the leader of the society Robert Zubrin, was that Elon Musk would attend it when he was not even invited. He gave a check for $5,000, which made everyone take notice. Before the dinner, Zubrin decided to invite Musk for coffee so that he could talk to him and know about his interest in the society as well as grill him if he knew what projects the society had underway.

After his interesting conversation with Musk, Zubrin decided to seat him at the VIP table with Carol Stoker and James Cameron, who were space buffs themselves. The four of them talked about various space investments and projects. While Musk had less knowledge about space, his interest in this area was deep, and this is why he ended up joining the Mars Society and donated $100,000!

During his conversation at the dinner, Musk decided to take one of the projects mentioned and do something different with it. His idea was to send mice to mars instead of the earth's orbit and see how long they could survive and procreate. He asked one of his friends if the idea was crazy but none of them replied with a straight face.

Musk had always felt that mankind was no longer pushing the boundaries of reality. To quieten his fears, he decided to browse NASA's website and see for himself what advances they were making. Instead of finding any kind of plans that would hint at an ongoing project, he found bupkis.

By now, Musk had amassed quite a bit of knowledge on space and had a large network of contacts in this industry. He started his space journey in hotel conference rooms. He would invite his contacts to airports, hotels, and various other places just to debate.

There was no formal business plan. He just wanted to talk about his "Mice to Mars" plan and see how other enthusiasts would react to it. All he wanted to do was make a grand gesture that would capture the world's attention. The price tag for these ideas was $20 million, and luminaires and scientists were brought together to figure out a way to do it.

Musk had a good thing going on so he resigned from the Mars Society and created his own called "Life to Mars Foundation." The type of people who attended the foundation's session was quite impressive. There was James Cameron along with some other celebrities, a scientist from NASA's Jet Propulsion Laboratory, Michael Griffin, and more.

Each person had their own knowledge about space. Griffin was the most qualified among them, having various credentials to his name. If there was someone who wants to fire something into space, it was Griffin. The best thing was that despite

Griffin's impressive background, he chose to work with Musk at his newfound company as the chief space thinker.

In 2005, Griffin was appointed as the head of NASA, and the company was thrilled to have someone who would contribute to the idea of space because they were fully invested in it. Both Musk and Griffin were on board with the idea to send mice into space and watch them hum down on the ground. Not exactly quality TV for us folks, but for Musk, it would be gold.

As the idea started to take shape, they realized that somewhere along the way, the project had taken a different turn. They were now pooling in ideas on something called "Mars Oasis." Based on this plan, Musk would shoot a rocket, a robotic greenhouse of sorts into Mars. Musk and a group of researchers started to make plans for producing oxygen on Mars. There were several technicalities involved, and for that reason, Musk wanted a rocket with a window and a camera to capture and send video feedback. First, some people were skeptical of the idea. However, as the plan proceeded, everyone started to take an interest. Their enthusiasm knew no bounds, and they even said that this idea could easily make Musk Time Magazine's "Man of the Year."

The only hurdle in the plan was budget. Musk had set aside around $30 million for the plan; however, that alone would be eaten up by the rocket. There were plenty of other things that weren't going according to plan because it all came down to the rocket. So, Musk decided to take a trip to Russia to buy a refurbished missile. Since he had no contacts in the country, he decided to get in touch with Jim Cantrell, who had done some work for the government of the United States. He had been put on house arrest by Russia due to a deal gone awry, and Musk could feel it in his bones that Cantrell was the guy who could get him what he wanted.

When Musk contacted Cantrell and made a shady arrangement, Cantrell thought that people from Russia were trying to kill him. So, he called him to a place where he couldn't pack a gun. When they both met, all the confusions were cleared, and Musk and Cantrell hit it off.

To cut a long story short, the deal with the Russians was a bust. On their way back, Musk turned to his team and said, "I think we can build the rocket ourselves."

Cantrell and Griffin were too drunk to make fun of Musk so they just stared at him as another millionaire who had lost his mind. However, when Musk showed them the plans, they were dumbfounded. He had detailed out the cost of parts carefully that would be needed to build the rocket as well as projections on how successful it would be in space.

Many people thought that Musk was another millionaire who would spend a good amount of money on building rockets, and when the engineers would get nowhere with the results, he would shut the project down. However, Musk was dedicated, and he needed someone on his team who was crazy about space and rockets. It was at John Garvey's workshop that Musk met Tom Mueller. He was just another kid from Idaho who had tinkered with machines and won a couple of science fairs to make his way to the big leagues.

Musk and Cantrell chatted, and the young man ended up joining Musk's team of space experts. That's when Musk decided to build his own space business. Griffin wanted to relocate, and when Musk rebuffed his request, he left the team. A few months later, Cantrell left the team stating that the entire project was too risky and costly.

In 2002, Musk founded Space Exploration Technologies, SpaceX for short. Plans were underway, and Musk and Mueller were working on the rockets when Musk's world upended. After a few days of his wife giving birth, Musk found his son dead in the crib. The loss was immense, and because of Musk's troubled past, he couldn't grieve. Musk's wife was distraught and started IVF treatments soon after. She then gave birth to twins and then a set of triplets.

By now, Musk had gotten things under control and threw himself into the daily grind of SpaceX. The initial deadline for launching the rocket was set somewhere in 2002. However, due to various technical problems, the launch didn't happen till 2006. As the rocket flew in the air, Musk watched from the control. After a few minutes, the rocket caught fire and started to spin. The rocket then flew straight down onto the launch pad and broke into pieces, with some of its parts falling into the reef. Several engineers wore diving gear to bring back the pieces, which were then placed in crates.

Blame for the failed launch was placed on an unnamed crew member, saying he didn't tighten some of the screws properly. After a thorough investigation, it was revealed that Jeremy Hollman, a young engineer on Musk's team, had worked last on the rocket. He was called into the office where he and Musk had a shouting match. When the rocket's parts were analyzed, it turned out they had been crusted with salt due to Kwaj's salty atmosphere. It was just one of those things that happened and couldn't be caught even after several tests. To this day, most engineers feel bad about how Hollman and his team members were treated.

In 2007, another rocket was launched, and it behaved properly for a few minutes. However, this time, the propellant was at fault, and the rocket burst into flames. None of this deterred Musk, and the whole process of building a rocket started again. During this time, Musk had several projects in the pipeline, which we will talk about briefly later.

In 2012, SpaceX finally made history when their Falcon 9 Rocket was launched. This time, there were no complications, and none of the components burst into flames. The spacecraft was sent to the International Space Station that carried supplies weighing 1,000 pounds for the astronauts working there.

In 2013, another spacecraft was launched that would attach itself to the earth's orbital part and match its rotation. By now, SpaceX had found its momentum, and they launched several other spacecraft in 2015, 2017, and 2018.

In late 2017, an updated design for his BFR, which Musk fondly called "The Big F***ing Rocket," was released. This rocket was designed to carry 100 people to Mars. His timeline for project completion was set in 2022. In an event, Musk announced that the BFR would conduct some short-term flights. Then, he talked about the previous delays in his project, which he believed wouldn't happen this time.

In 2018, SpaceX got permission from the US government to launch several satellites that would reach the low orbit and provide internet services. This satellite was named *Starlink* and later on became the best broadband service accessible for rural areas.

**The Story of Tesla** began in 2003. A chemistry wiz named J.B. Straubel would come up with crazy ideas from time to time and conduct experiments that would put his life in danger. The 2-inch long scar on his face was proof of his experiments' riskiness. His main interest was in solar power for vehicles. At the time, none of the companies in the world had come up with such an idea.

By 2002, Straubel had not only tried building his own electric car but also bounced around from a motor company to another. During one of these job shifts, Straubel came into contact with his Stanford solar car team. They had been secretly working on a project to make an electric vehicle that would run on solar power. Though Stanford had tried to close down the project, the students had insisted they need no help from the university. Straubel helped them build vehicles, and they would compete in races. He even went as far as inviting them to their place to stay.

A conversation at night after a race had them talking about how lithium batteries had performed better in a car. He pitched his idea about using lithium batteries to the Stanford group, and they all said they would be on board if he could come up with the funding for it.

So, Straubel stalked investors for money shamelessly. It was during one of his campaigns when Harold Rosen took Straubel with him to talk with Musk. The young man pitched his idea about an electric plane but got no response from Musk. However, when he talked about electric vehicles, the idea struck a chord with Musk.

Musk himself had been thinking about creating electric vehicles for years. When he heard Straubel's idea of using lithium batteries, he was all in. Musk gave Straubel $10,000 of the $100,000 he was looking for and formed a great kinship over their shared interest.

To impress him further, Straubel asked the President of AC Propulsion a tzero for Musk to drive. Musk fell in love with the car and tried to commercialize it. However, the engineers at AC Propulsion wouldn't agree to the deal. Musk then decided to go his own way.

Unbeknownst to Straubel, two business partners Martin Eberhard and Marc Tarpenning were working on their own project of electric-powered vehicles. In 2003, a company was incorporated, which was named Tesla. The partners, along with other investors, had the skills and knowledge to run a company and make cars. Now, they needed proper backing from someone who knew his way around such projects. In their minds, they had one name: Elon Musk.

Since Musk was already looking for a way in, he was eager to meet the Eberhard and Tarpenning. Once he heard what they had to say, he was on board. After the meeting, Musk immediately called Straubel and told him to go meet the guys. Through Straubel was a bit skeptical because he had never heard about Eberhard and Tarpenning, he still paid them a visit. He told them about the batteries he had been working on, and Straubel was hired on the spot.

Musk had now joined forces with business partners and hired some ambitious engineers. Now, everyone started working on "Roadster," the first car that Tesla would build. They had no idea what was in store for them. During this time, Musk faced many issues. Most of his engineers were still in Kwaj, working on the Falcon for SpaceX. Tesla had now become a huge company with hundreds of employees. Building a sports car was no easy task, and the engineers dealt with the same problems as the ones they did when starting with Falcon.

Employees at Tesla saw another side of Musk when the first Roadster failed. People were yelled at, kicked out of meetings, and fired on the spot, even those who had done an awesome job in the past. No one was safe from Musk's wrath. On a personal level, Musk was struggling with Justine and her blog, and on a professional level, he couldn't seem to catch a break with his inventions.

During this time, Musk also became an inspiration for the movie Iron Man. When Robert Downey Jr. got wind of such a man who was exactly like his character Tony Stark, he decided to pay a visit to the SpaceX headquarters. They both hit it off, and Musk had a great time chatting with someone who knew something about technology. When Downey began filming, he asked Jon Favreau, the director of Iron Man, to place a Tesla Roadster in the movie. On a superficial level, he wanted to convey that Tony was such a cool character that he had a Roadster before it even came out. Musk began to enjoy his associations with celebrities, and he and Justine were invited to many Hollywood events and weddings.

The struggle of building the perfect Roadster continued. It was in 2008 when Tesla finally unveiled the car that was capable of accelerating to 60 mph in just 3.7 seconds and could cover a distance of 250 miles.

By now, Daimler had a stake in Tesla and Musk had struck a partnership with Toyota. Eventually, Tesla's public offering started in 2010 and raised $226 million. In 2008, Tesla announced a new car, known as the Model S, which would be the first electric sedan created by the company. The car was finally introduced in 2012 and 2013, and Motor Trend Magazine awarded it as "The Car of the Year."

In 2017, Tesla had surpassed General Motors and became the most valuable carmaker in the US. Musk was immensely impressed with this progress and ramped up the production for the Model 3 sedan. By now, Musk was on a roll, and things were going well. In 2019, a Model S four-door sedan set the highest speed record in Monterey County, California at the Laguna Seca Raceway. The Model 3 sedan was finally introduced to the public in 2019 at a price tag of $35,000, which was way less than the $69,500 for Model X and S electric sedans.

In 2019, the Semi-Truck was announced after countless delays, and in the same year, Model Y, Tesla's much-awaited card was unveiled too. The car was available for buying in 2020. This model could reach 60 mph in just 3.5 seconds and covered a range of 300 miles. This isn't the end of Tesla models and Musk promises to release more technology-rich cars that will make human lives easier.

## The Musk Who Is More Than Just Tesla and SpaceX

Musk is now more than just a name. It's a brand that promises innovation. PayPal, Tesla, and SpaceX are not the only businesses that Musk built, sold and controls. He has a couple of other small businesses that most people don't know about, such as SolarCity, which was acquired in 2016. The company is dedicated to advancing and promoting sustainable energy products.

He also launched The Boring Company in 2017. This company builds tunnels to reduce road and street traffic. There are several inventions to his name as well, some of which are still in progress. People can find out more about them online. Most of these inventions are targeted at improving human life.

From these stories, one of the things you might have learned is that Musk is a go-getter. He believes in doing things with a plan and sometimes, just likes to jump in. His exacting and controlling nature has caused many problems, like being taken down from the CEO position. However, with his hard work and dedication, he built another company from scratch — one that was even better than previous ones.

Today, Musk is constantly in the news not just because of his wealth but also because of the empires he has built. Moreover, his plans to colonize Mars and his constant talk about how AI will take over the world and control humans as pets is something that is not sitting well with people.

## The Secrets Behind Elon Musk's Success

*"Failure is an option here. If things are not failing, you are not innovating enough."*

When you think about one of the most innovative billionaires in the world, the name Elon Musk pops into your mind.

Disruptor. Trendsetter, Game changer… these are all words synonymous with Musk. His most noticeable and talked about accomplishments are Tesla, SpaceX, and PayPal. For Musk, an ordinary day in the office includes trying to launch another rocket or building another Tesla model.

He's the real-life Iron Man, who commits himself fully to the ideas in his mind. Unlike other billionaires, Musk has lost his money and made billions more, and that too multiple times with different businesses.

As 2021 began, Musk was the wealthiest man in the world, a spot he keeps competing for with Jeff Bezos and Bernard Arnault. Musk has even made it to the list of Time Magazine's 100 Most Influential People. Musk and his success continue to grow every time he comes up with something new. So, what is the secret behind it?

Let's find out:

## Give Your Best and Work Like Hell

*"Starting and growing a business is as much about the innovation, drive, and determination of the people behind it as the product they sell."*

Musk's work ethic is fierce. When he and his brother were working in PayPal, they lived in the office. They ate there, slept there, and took showers at the YMCA. They were so dedicated to building a company that nothing was off-limits. So, they worked like hell and put in 100 hours every week.

Musk believes that it was his dedication that improved his odds of success. His reasoning behind his work ethic was if people are putting in 40 hours and you are working double that time then you will achieve your goal in 4 months, whereas it will take others 1 year to achieve the same thing.

## Be Passionate About What You Do

*"People work better when they <u>know what the goal is and why</u>. It is important that people look forward to coming to work in the morning and enjoy working. P<u>ursue what you are passionate about</u>. That will make you happier than pretty much anything else"*

Every idea that Musk came up with, was because of his interest in that area. Having worked in banks, he knew how they were struggling with debt, and that gave him the idea to start PayPal. With SpaceX, his interest in Mars was the driving factor, and it evolved to producing sustainable energy. All these ventures were started on a whim had been well-researched on were backed by passion.

## Don't Follow the Trend

*"I don't create companies for the sake of creating companies, but to get things done."*

For Musk, it was never about creating a brand. His interest was more in coming up with solutions for current world problems.

He is a trendsetter so he does not believe in following a trend. All of Musk's companies solve problems, competing in industries with fewer players or no players at all.

When PayPal was founded, it was the only company that allowed people to transfer money through email. SpaceX is the very first company in the world to send its spacecraft called Dragon to ISS. Lastly, Tesla is the best and foremost electric car company in the world.

To reap bigger and better rewards, you need to focus on innovation. The competition will automatically diminish if your idea is unique. Where there's a monopoly, there's plenty of room to be innovative where profits are higher.

## Do Something Important

*"I always have optimism, but I'm realistic. It was not with the expectation of great success that I started Tesla or SpaceX... It's just that <u>I thought they were important</u> enough to do anyway."*

Musk didn't start SpaceX or Tesla just because he came up with an innovative idea. He was truly concerned about where today's world was going. He knew that if people continued to take the resources available to them for granted, no one would ever move forward, and the future would look the same.

In his late 20s, Musk had more money than he had ever imagined. He could have easily retired and lived a cushy life. However, he pressed on kept working. To him, work had more importance than just creating money. It was more about changing the world. So, be bold and choose something important to you.

## Read to Lead

*"How did you learn to build rockets?" Musk: "I read books."*

Self-education never ends! You can't possibly know everything, but you sure can try. As a kid, Musk read the whole Encyclopedia Britannica. While today's generation is busy creating memes and reading social media posts, Musk's younger self-set a reading trend.

Wise people know that getting lost in a good book is the best way to expand your horizons. Reading won't only give you new ideas but insights that will change the way you think. Musk believes that a fast learner is a great earner.

## Never Shy Away from Constructive Criticism

*"I think it's very important to have a feedback loop, where you're constantly thinking about what you've done and how you could be doing it better."*

While Musk was known for his temper, which would make any employee fear for their job, he was not the kind of person who took action without thinking about it first. Yes, he made plenty of mistakes when SpaceX was being established, such as firing engineers who weren't at fault. However, in the name of success, he would do anything, and that included taking constructive criticism. If a problem occurred on his watch, he wanted answers and suggestions on how to fit.

Many CEOs and people in leadership roles don't like to be told what they are doing wrong. They see it as an insult. In contrast, Musk always sought valuable advice from his trusted people and friends. Before starting a new venture that he knew people would respond to skeptically, he would ask his friends if he was insane to even think of such a thing.

If the criticism or negative feedback has an underlying reason that does not make sense, tell people to adjust their behavior. Musk says that he's not perfect but soliciting negative feedback, something a sane person won't do, is how he works. According to him, if the suggestion is coming from a friend, they have your best interest at heart.

## Attract Great People

*"My biggest mistake is probably weighing too much on someone's talent and not someone's personality. I think it matters whether someone has a good heart."*

Musk still thinks about the time when the control of Zip2 was taken away from him. Then, there was the time when a coup was started to kick Musk out of PayPal. The one thing that Musk learned during both these ventures was that never trust someone based on their talent. Sure, they can get the job done better than anyone else but do they have a good heart? Do you know about their intentions? Do you think they will stab in you the back at the first opportunity they get?

A company is made by a group of people dedicated to one goal. Even if these people have the same vision, find out if they are loyal too. Musk made the mistake of being in the advisory role in his first two ventures. After that, he always held the largest stake in his company so that no one could push him out.

## Take Risks or Else Life Will Get in the Way

How many times have your loved ones said that there will be time to make your career but a family should always come first?

Musk believes in the opposite. His thinking is that once you get a family, it becomes harder to prioritize and your loved ones always get in the middle of you and your dreams. You can't shy away from obligations. However, if you want to be successful in your career, you need to choose yourself first!

Do not see this as a selfish act. Some things can slow you down in life. So, take a risk and do what you think is best for you. If that means focusing all your energy and time on your career, so be it.

## Be Extremely Tenacious



One of Musk's greatest mistakes was that he failed to understand where the other person was coming from. His focus caused him to not know about the other things that happened under his nose;  Musk believes that hiring a nice person is the key to managing a company because they will be as focused as you.

If you look up the definition of "tenacious" in the dictionary, you will see it explained as an adjective: *not readily relinquishing a position, principle, or course of action; determined*.

Even when Tesla and SpaceX were about to be bankrupt, Musk stuck to his vision and pushed as hard as he could! He used the payout from PayPal and invested almost all of it into the two companies to make sure none of the projects experienced any delays, they were already having.

Yes, Musk was exacting and rude at times. However, his ideas didn't just come off the top of his head. They were well-thought-out with graphs and statistics.

## Consider What's the Worst That Could Happen

*"Persistence is very important. You should not give up unless you are forced to give up."*

Back when Musk was starting his entrepreneurial journey, which was at the age of 17, he decided to conduct a little experiment to see if he could live with as little as possible. So, every day, he ate oranges and hot dogs that cost $1. He was living a dollar a day, which meant that the person he was buying from was earning $30 from him alone. That didn't seem too hard.

Musk didn't do this because he was poor. At one point in his life, he simply wanted to know if he lost all his money, what would happen.

According to Musk, this is how an entrepreneur should live, one who is dedicated to making it. Of course, he has been successful and made millions. However, he knew what it felt like to be poor, and this thinking was reflected in the business decisions he took. He never invested money in anything that he didn't believe in. Moreover, he never approved a request for buying something until and unless it was necessary.

## Sex Sells

Say, what?

You are probably wondering what sex has to do with any of Musk's creations. The truth is that sex sells and if you know the right marketing techniques, you can use this tip to take yourself to the top.

If you take a look at the Tesla cars, you will notice that they all have sexual undertones. Musk is not only creative but has a unique sense of humor. Tesla introduced three of its car one after the other with different model names. The first one was S, then came X and the last one was Model 3, which was represented by three horizontal lines. Initially, the model was named E. Put the names of all the models together and you get one word: SEX.

Later on, Tesla introduced the D dual motor. In the unveiling ceremony, Musk joked about the model, and in the background, you could hear a fan saying, *"Show us your D"* to which Musk good-naturedly replied, *"You will notice my pants have Velcro seams."*

## Invest Your Profits



Musk has never shied away from investing his money in ventures that he whole heartedly believes in. His first two companies were cashed in for millions of dollars, and each time, he used at least 45% of the earnings and invested them into a new business within the year.

- On the sale of Zip2, Musk made $22 million. He used $10 million and found X.com, which was later named PayPal.
- On the sale of PayPal, Musk made $165 million. He used $100 million and found SpaceX.
- Musk also invested in SolarCity (20,724,991) and Tesla Motors (33,076,212).

The ownership of SolarCity, SpaceX, and Tesla are the three companies that make most of Musk's billion dollars wealth.

## Innovate to the Point Where You Are Considered the Best

*"There are really two things that have to occur in order for a new technology to be affordable. One is you need economies of scale. The other is <u>you need to iterate on the design</u>. You need to go through a few versions."*

In 2015, Consumer Reports tweeted, "Breaking: Tesla P85D is the best car we've tested in 80 years of testing cars." #carofthefuture

This is the type of acknowledgment you need to boost your product's image. However, to reach this point, you need to give your best and all to your product, and Musk did exactly that.

## Know Your Limits

Musk is the hardest and smartest working entrepreneur in the 21st century. However, he too is a human being, and he can only work so many hours. With 5 boys and a wife, he needs to divide his time between his family and work. Tesla and SpaceX take up most of his time, and Musk knew that taking on another company would be too much for him.

Even though he was still full of ideas, some quite good that would bring a lot of change in the world, he decided to wait before jumping with both feet in. When he founded SolarCity, he knew that he wouldn't be able to oversee its working every day. So, he shared the idea with his cousins Lyndon and Peter Rive, who agreed to manage the company. Since Musk had already been burned too many times in the past, he knew that he would have to have some kind of hold over the company, and thus, he became its principal investor.

## Conclusion

Like every other entrepreneur, Musk saw his fair share of struggles. A lack of business acumen resulted in Musk losing his first company because he identified more as an engineer rather than a CEO. Later on, he realized that if he wanted to be a successful businessman, he would have to wear both caps.

Though Musk's advice on how to be successful is plenty, his most notable one would be to improvise. Musk liked to read books so knew multiple ways to go about a problem. He knew that failure is and would always be an option. He feared an outcome that would not be to his liking but that didn't stop him from doing what he wanted to do. He simply tried to minimize his fear so that it wouldn't interfere with his thought process.

There are many instances where Musk did not let small things delay his projects. For a millionaire, using private jets or an island for his personal use wasn't anything big. When SpaceX needs more room to launch their rockets, Musk found an island to make it happen. He once flew in his private jet to France just to deliver a machine tool that would help speed up production.

Perhaps his most unique improvise moment was when he hired a truck with a refrigerator because a Tesla prototype needed to be tested in the cold. They say, "Where there's a will, there's a way," and no one knows this better than Musk.

Musk has a tendency of pissing off people because he has his fingers in too many pies. Following is a glimpse of what Musk is working on, which has raised the competition bar so high that people are afraid to step into any industry that is led by this billionaire:

|  | Industry | How It's Disrupting the Industry |
|---|---|---|
| **SpaceX** | Space Launches | Offering transport to space at a low price |
|  | Telecommunications | Offering cheap service |
|  | Satellite Internet | Putting up more space satellites that are cheaper |
| **Tesla** | Automobiles | Building the lowest-cost and best electric vehicles |
|  | Personal Transport | Eliminating car ownership entirely |
|  | Solar Energy | Increasing access with Solar Roof and Powerwall |
|  | Fossil Fuels | Maximizing solar panels efficiency |
|  | Car Sharing | Making Tesla cars available to the public via an app |
| **The Boring Company** | Tunneling | Reducing underground tunneling cost |
|  | Infrastructure | Building efficient transportation infrastructure |
|  | Real Estate | Offering people houses within close distance to work |
|  | Freight Shipping | Using magnitude to reduce freight costs |
| **OpenAI** | AI/Machine Learning | Creating the world's best AI system |
|  | Competitive Gaming | Producing better AIs consistently |

| **Neuralink** | Prosthetics | Using magnitude to reduce the cost of prostheses |
| | Medicine (Treatment) | Using simple injections to treat serious illness |
| | Military | Enhancing human capabilities |
| | Robotics | Building a better model for brain-machine interaction |

As you can see, whoever dares to step into Musk's world, will be crushed immediately by his brilliant mind and award-winning team of engineers.

Now that you have gotten to know who and what Musk is, you will be able to relate to his advice on getting to the top. His journey was full of betrayal, heartbreak, and hard work. It took him years to get where he is today but he made it. Most people say, "Try and try again until you don't succeed." Musk truly understands this because he has walked the walk and talked the talk. He NEVER gave up, which is what has made him the richest man in the world.